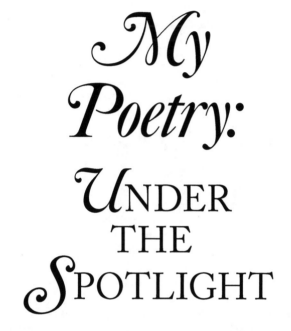

My Poetry: UNDER THE SPOTLIGHT

TERRANCE J. WILLIAMSON

WESTBOW
PRESS®
A DIVISION OF THOMAS NELSON
& ZONDERVAN

This book is a work of non-fiction. Unless otherwise noted, the author
and the publisher make no explicit guarantees as to the accuracy of
the information contained in this book and in some cases, names of
people and places have been altered to protect their privacy.

WestBow Press books may be ordered through booksellers or by contacting:

WestBow Press
A Division of Thomas Nelson & Zondervan
1663 Liberty Drive
Bloomington, IN 47403
www.westbowpress.com
844-714-3454

ISBN: 979-8-3850-0833-9 (sc)
ISBN: 979-8-3850-0835-3 (hc)
ISBN: 979-8-3850-0834-6 (e)

Library of Congress Control Number: 2023918143

Print information available on the last page.

WestBow Press rev. date: 10/27/2023

Dedicated to Detrick Coleman A.K.A. Yusuf who got this ball to rollin, aint no stopping it now!

Thank you, Brother, and Friend.

$\mathcal{I}$NTRODUCTION

At one point of time or another, we've all been plagued and have faced different forms of darkness, in our lives. Yet for the slightest glimmer of light, we can find a reason to carry on. I found out that even when facing the harsh reality of prison walls, shackles, and chains, there is hope. This dramatic theme screams and echoes loudly throughout these pages.

However, within your own journey through the mine fields of darkness, just as mine, you can find so much more. Metaphorically speaking, life is full of unexpected explosions. The key thing is how we choose to deal with them once they go off.

Therefore, whether through the murky waters of shame or the glittering streams of glory, I simply desire to share my experience. I have so much hope to reach others over the distant winds with the power of spirit and truth. I pray that you will sift out something valuable as you examine this poetic text. Something worthy to make a difference and create more meaning in your life. Wanting to redeem the time, my greatest hope is to repay darkness in everlasting light.

If there was a key to the door of light, I would walk through and lock away all the darkness. T.J.W.

CONTENTS

*T*HIN ICE

Standing on thin ice,
so cold I am bound to freeze,
let alone breathe.
Why, the life we live,
we often fall in,
so quick to end
before we even begin.
You'll never be perfect
and hardly complete,
but if you listen,
you can hear the cracks beneath your feet. Ω

DEEPER THOUGHTS EMERGE

…I didn't. Darkness swept, and I fell deep. Summer must have been on another
plane of existence, for I was lost, swallowed within the deepest depths of winter
and its frigid distance.
Behold, a foolish mind trapped in its own realm of resistance.
How can anyone consciously see if he or she continuously walks the path of the
blind?
By the cold I was paralyzed. By the cold I was sinking into what seemed to be an
unwakeable sleep.

But the truth is, that reality really speaks!
All the chaotic choices I was carelessly
willing to make found me in situations
and places I never could imagine. Without a doubt, I had many hopes and
dreams, but the fruitless life
I lived, well, that was just wishful thinking.   Ω

*W*ISHFUL THINKING

I thought many things in life,
but I found these things
would turn out quite different.

I thought I would live up to
my dreams of fortune and fame,
but I found the nightmare of being
broken, so broken
that my shoulders fall weak,
carrying such burdens of shame.

I thought I would be in love forever,
but I found hatred
has a cruel way of being clever,
the great division of together.

I thought I would have happiness forever
and always in my heart
and so my eyes,
but I found tears can't help
but to rain down as I cry an
endless river that never
seems to dry.

Why, Oh, why?
Can anybody advise?
Please specify.
For an answer, I'm standing by.
I know plenty can sympathize
as they, too, question,
why, oh, why?

And it doesn't stop there—
the dark thickness is in the air.
So once again as I expel
these false thoughts from within,
let me begin.

I thought I would have true friends
who would last until the grave,
but I found before a season's freshly picked
funeral flowers could rise,
they had already died away,
like the sun does each day.
Yet never to return, O yesterday.
I thought I would know freedom,
a paradise before the serpent
entered the garden of Eden.
But I found prison walls,
shackles, and silver chains.
Guards watching my every step,
for I no longer have a right to anything,
not even my own name.

I thought life would be pleasant,
if not perfect, even plain,
but in the least bit surely worth it.
But I found sorrows, shame,

betrayal, blame,
punishment, and so much pain.
I fell into failure-
what a burn of this internal flame.

Sadly, I thought many things in life,
but I found these things
would turn out quite different.

However, this is life,
although it's easier said than done,
but no matter what I thought,
this is how I am living.   Ω

BROKEN

Dreams fall, unfold, and crash
in the middle of the road.
What a collision to the skull.
I deeply wish to wake up,
but I don't want to die slow.   Ω

$\mathcal{A}$FRAID TO SPEAK

There I was –
standing in front of everybody,
but my voice could not speak.
I was frightened, broken, and so, so weak.
Worried about what others think.
Sadly, I was suffering in my own defeat.
Why, when it was my moment to shine,
I was afraid to speak.   Ω

$\mathscr{I}$T KILLED EVERYTHING

I tried to run,
but low self-esteem caught me.
It killed everything-
all my desires, all my dreams.
For when I thought to take flight,
I remembered my broken wings.

I tried to run,
but low self-esteem caught me.
It killed everything-
who I was and all it should mean;
it stole my identity.
For when I looked in the mirror
my image was wiped clean.
Where I became all that,
they wanted me to be.
UGLY, HORRIBLE, FOOLISH,
and don't forget WEAK.

I tried to run,
but low self-esteem caught me.
It killed everything-
THE HORROR!
THE HORROR!

A horrific sight filled my eyes,
as it paints the scene.

So hurt and confused by the truth,
my reality blurred.
So affected I believed every cruel word
that my heart submerged.
I wasn't crumbled
but crushed by their deadly words.
Hate and abuse on a unstinting purge,
dinning on my soul like
a parasitic creature eating at my nerves.
I tried to run,
but low self-esteem caught me.
It killed everything.   Ω

DARKNESS

With nowhere to end or nowhere to start,
darkness fills my eyes and so my heart.
If my body is one whole,
then why do I feel so torn apart?

Darkness –
it is there, so it is here,
so, so near, closer than the deepest of fears.
I'm so alone when many people are here,
but they are not worth my voice,
because I'm not worth their ears.
Either I'm invisible or they are blind.
Neither is true,
although it works for my mind.

This darkness is not my desired home,
still I'm trapped here like a terrible scar
once the stitches are gone.

This darkness is not my desired home.
Bright are the world's days,
yet in me, no light has shown.
I wonder why?
What have I done?

Why does the light of life
seem so on the run?

Darkness –
I hate it, but I can take it,
for I have done it for so long.

With nowhere to end or nowhere to start
this darkness is not my desired home,
however, since I'm here, I have no choice
but to accept it as my very own.   Ω

$\mathcal{I}$ COULD NOT FEEL

I have many regrets.
Daily I desperately wish
I could shake them off like no sweat.
However, I'm caught in Consequence's
and Judgment's relentless net.
I desire to break their hold,
but no matter how hard I try,
exhaustion takes me.
Death, O death,
I nearly could die.
Sleepless nights I've cried
as Time's hourglass spills,
for deep within my thoughts
the truth has been revealed.
"Drugs Numb and Kill your reality"
I could not feel.
I was numb.
I could not feel
while I was trapped in Evil's folds.
I could not feel.
I can see it all clearly now.
After the high.
Death, O death,
I nearly could die.   Ω

$\mathcal{M}$Y NEWS REPORT

Lady distant in the wind -
I'm not a meteorologist, though, I sadly report,
causing you pain brought me pleasure.

Miserable was the weather-
your daily storms, earthquakes, and hurricanes.
When a forecast couldn't be explained,
behind all your disasters,
I'm the only one to blame.

Lady distant in the wind -
I am so sorry in every degree you had to meet a mind dark,
clouded by a thunderstorm with a slight chance of rain. Ω

JUST CAN'T LET GO

Lost in a tasteless disaster.
Memories are like ghost
haunting me ever-after.
Desperately, I want to run,
but I've already been captured,
and so the darkness
just gets thicker and blacker.
Then how on earth
can I let my past troubles go?
They're of me,
like someone who deeply loves me.
All about me,
as if they can't live without me;
so clingy and unrousing.
I'd say I could live without them
like needless candlelights,
you snuff out.
Then barrel through the dark haze
to seek out and take on
new attributes of such meaningful character.
But just as I'd say
I could live without them,
you can see clearly,
here we are,

wings of a flock together.
However, look at you,
always judging others
with a plank wedged in your eye.
You aren't even a bird but
are full of feathers.
A man and his mind
and what he will mind.
Haunted by memories of his
very own written history,
he just can't let go.   Ω

DARK NIGHT

On my dark nights,
I could have used a friend to get me right.
Why, hope wasn't there.
I felt fear and its big brother fright.
On my dark nights,
I was lost without a way, without a light.
I could have made do with anything
to get me out this darkness.
A simple flash of the headlights.
Why, to see only for a second
is a moment to get my head clear,
to get my head right.
It would have meant everything
for this was my life.
Now on my clear days
I suffer the foul pains.
THE PRICE
of my past dark nights
because it's far too late.
It could have meant everything
to make a difference.
Why, this is my life.   Ω

ALONE IN THE DARKNESS

Deep within the night's midst, shrouded by darkness,
the lonely wolf howls horridly at the moon,
lost in his torment, lost in his doom.
No longer a man,
for his soul has been consumed.
Torn away like an unwanted child,
snatched from its mother's womb.
Lonely are his days, cold like the headstone of a grave.

Deep within the night's midst, shrouded by darkness.
Alone, helpless, with no hope.
A laugh at Life's cruel joke.
Clad in fear, a desire to burn then smoke,
though death won't strike.
For this fire is forever trapped inside,
only hatred can ignite.
So blind that flame,
Has he ever seen love's light?

Deep within the night's midst, shrouded by darkness,
there is pain, for he isn't completely heartless.
He is willing to make do
and claim what he can out of darkness.
Something old, something new,

something borrowed, something blue.
Lost in his torment, lost in his doom,
he wants what he knows he can't have.
He wants what he believes would make living
his horrid life not so bad.
It is always on his mind
but out of his grasp.
He could run, dash, even sprint,
but it's beyond fast.
Only the darkness he can catch;
only the darkness he will clash.
He will go over the mountains, over the hills.
Alone he shall travel against his will.

Deep within the Night's midst, shrouded by darkness,
The lonely wolf howls horridly at the moon.
He is hurt, but there's no physical womb.
Sorrow flows over his rugged fur coat.
He can only scratch,
for his claws can't stroke
These memories that are far from a blur.
His ears stand on end
to what they once were.

Deep within the Night's midst, shrouded by the darkness.
Are these troubling thoughts deep within his conscience,
Then was he not forever haunted?
Did he once have a chance
but chose the darkness to dance?
And if so, can he once again change
or is the beast ever more in his veins.
So untamed the wolf wildly remains,
shrouded by darkness with only himself to blame.   Ω

*W*ALKING BLIND

Time has passed me by,
A mournful death, but I haven't died.
Stuck in past, shattered memories,
It's so hard to look to an unknown future.

Time has passed me by,
I desperately wish to catch it,
Yet my access is denied,
Unless it's in my dreams
I close my eyes
I guess this is why I always
Talk about darkness.

Time has passed me by,
and I'm walking blind.   Ω

$\mathcal{F}$EAR

Inspired by: Gwendolyn Brooks and Maya Angelou

Don't whip me, beat nor break me.
You have held onto me far too long.
Before the shackles,
by you,
I had already been arrested.
They say you bring hatred. And I question,
"Is this why I've chosen all these dark paths, in my past?"
I would say I've gotten rid of you,
But that's like a fisherman saying
He was never after a great bass.
I confess, you have clothed me
And been living in my heart,
That you show up clearly in my eyes.
I could walk many ways,
But the truth doesn't lie.
You have held on to me for far too long.
I desire to fly,
But you have overwhelming gravity control.
I know, I know there will be a chance to escape,
But that's only if I can strip you and brake
Your dreadful hold and free my soul.   Ω

*T*HE PRICE

Pen-Sword of Victory

Days are cold and just get colder.
When there's no closer as they constantly turn over.
People steady die as you just get old and older,
Waiting to Croke over.
I don't have a nickel,
Let alone a dime,
But this is the price of life,
Especially when you're doing time. Ω

$\mathcal{S}$ECURUS

Sometimes when life seems on the edge
And one suffers deeply
from a lack of daily bread
because emptiness, sorrows, and loneliness
are all that's feed.
Death O' Death –
Surely, I hoped to live,
But they were eating me ALIVE.
Death O' Death God knows I could have DIED.
For though I desperately wanted to survive
They broke my window pane of resistance.
Yet cracked, crushed, dust particles
Adding up to not much,
it was there-
Out over in the distance,
A light sustained my hunger,
A light so sufficient vanquished all hunger pains like
I was suddenly dinning in Love's Kitchen.
It was there and then I realized
That when life seems on the edge
And there is nothing,
sometimes a simple voice
Can make all the difference.   Ω

$\mathscr{A}$ CHANGE IN DIET

Debauchery lies at these gates
And between these animalistic like bars.
Discontentment swells within disturbed souls
And continues to evolve.
It is easy to induce for it is the norm
And plays its demonic use.
Behold the power to channel chaos,
Destruction, and the true meaning of abuse.
I admit I have an unusual hunger, a tremendous appetite.
And yet I no longer can stomach such a plight.
Pure darkness swepts and lines every corner
Masking many faces like that of medieval knights.
O' how imperative it is to evade such
and to endeavor to find the slightest crack
to be unveiled within the light.
I admit I have an unusual hunger,
A tremendous appetite
To no longer be conflicted,
But for once in my life
To try and do something right.   Ω

ℐN MAXIMUM SECURITY PRISON (THE PIT)

Dedicated to brothers and sisters who have been through
and know the struggles of living in a maximum penitentiary.
Keep your head up!

Winter O' Winter is not even near
Yet darkness and cold
Are chipping at my soul,
And so my ears,
And even worse, I can see it eating
And tearing away at my peers.
It is drunk, fueled by our intense hatred
And our deepest pits of fears.
It is more worse
Than the bleak absence of light,
For this darkness has a more deadly bite.
It snaps and chokes out
Any means or sense of hope.

30-50-100-NATURAL LIFE.
A man is nothing without his family,
A man is nothing without his kids and wife.

30-50-100-NATURAL LIFE.
The courts should lighten up, but, OVERRULLED!
They don't take that advice.

30-50-100-NATURAL LIFE.
Never to see the light of day,
Why, darkness surely washes that thought away.
Broken spirit-
So wicked and loud,
In silence you can hear it.
Yet the darkness and cold
Continue to fester and mold.

GRIM, EVIL, TOXIC are the minds.
With no hope, there's no wonder why
Within these walls people are dying.
GRIM, EVIL, TOXIC are the minds.
I have to wake up
And stop walking blind.
Because even when I want no part of this,
I am there in the midst,
Choking on mace or ducking a fist,
Running away or going forward like a gorilla thinking,
"HELP ME LORD!
Because I better not miss.
BOOM!!!
BANG!!!
Shotguns pump, heart beats hit.
One-man cries as another man piss
He is scared, I am too,
But they tell us to get on the ground
Or the next shot belongs to you-
So, we all freeze facedown,
Stuck like super glue.

Broken spirit-
All this happened out of the blue.
It is over, cuff go on,
Officer's guns go down.
Segregation or back to the cell,
We are all on lockdown.

Winters O' Winter is not ever near,
But the horrendous heat of the summer must playout.
Collect calls on the phone to my cuz like,
"Man, STAYOUT!"
I want to put a caution sign up
Cause once you're locked in,
It seems like there's no way out.
I question; what do you do
When you're tried of putting up your fist
And you don't want to make a knife?
And if you thought to go to P.C.
My friend, even that comes with a price.
I haven't been there one day
And I won't be going tonight.

It is over,
But the craze of the crazy still ignites,
Cause even now two cells over
I hear two men fight.
The darkness and cold
Are chipping at my soul,
But I find it ironically funny
How I feel for another man's life-

Drunk off hatred I find myself sobered.
Yet a fool of fools I am to think
Such chaos could really be over.

For whether in the chow hall, yard or cell,
This creation of darkness is nothing new.

Broken Spirit-
Why, this is what men with
30-50-100-NATURAL LIFE DO.   Ω

JONAH 2:6

I went down to the moorings of the mountains.
The earth with its bars closed behind me forever.
Yet you have brought up my life from the pit,
O Lord, My God.   Ω

A DIFFERENT STORY

Weak in the pen
I became wicked with the pen.
Strengthen by powerful words,
With God's gift I dug my way out
From the catastrophic cave in.

It's funny how
When I became trapped behind bars,
I was released by these bars
Lined up before me.
Life looks up,
And now I can tell a different story.   Ω

ℰCHOES OF DEFEAT

Defeat is surely a burden,
Especially when any kill is considered certain.
For there's no hope to survive
Even if you had America's top surgeon.

Defeat is surely a burden,
Especially when it's drawn out in humiliation
When you would rather prefer mercy,
And the end to be urgent.

Defeat is surely a burden,
Especially when any kill is considered certain.
But I hardly know how to submit
And be its helpful servant.   Ω

*M*Y SOUL DAY

written October 26, 2017

The heat may rise,
The fire may fly,
Hot like coals, at any moment
One could die.
Yet head above water, I am alive.
If ever there was a drug,
I'm hooked to survive.
At 32 I do more than strive,
Trapped 11 years within these walls, I thrive
And I give all glory
And praise to the Lord Most High.   Ω

£ETTER TO FREEDOM

(Featuring Kanye)

Dear Freedom, Date: Present

Meet me in the distance. Away from shackles, away from chains, away from poverty and being another man's gain. Away from the color code and societies standard and belief of life on the totem pole. Away from drug abuse and the likes of a broken soul.

Away, far away from mental bondage and settling for things whose worth are no more than peer garbage. Away from the setbacks of somebody else in which I will greatly suffer from and be held hostage.

Freedom, meet me in the distance. I would truly like to meet with you. Not as a playdate, a fling, nor to misuse and abuse you, but to really get to know you, and you to get to know me too.

I have no doubt and believe if given a chance, we would be a wonderful fit together. I know that it has been said that you are not meant for me nor my people, but please don't fall for their wicked lies. Why, you would look so good on me. Then, and only then I could be nothing short of magnificent wrapped in your long, flowing cloak of independence. Maybe they fear I will rise and be crowned King. Yet if that's what you have in store for me, then so be it.

Nevertheless, father stretch my hands, because I just want to feel liberated, and live the life of Pablo. Freedom, I see you coming, meet me in the distance.

You are my future, be with me through life and all eternity. It's funny how I barely know you, but I love you. You have my heart.

Truly yours,

Terrance J.
P.S. Come to Life, write me back soon!   Ω

No SIGNS OF MAIL

O'mail man, please don't pass me by,
Don't you know I want a letter or two,
Just like these other guys?
I have gone days, even weeks,
But never months where my name
You fail to speak.

O'mail man, please don't pass me by.
Darkness has always flooded my quarters,
But mail has always offered
The slightest shimmer of light,
Even those built on false hope,
Those that easily fall into
A rubble of lies.

O'mail man, please don't pass me by,
Although they appear to be just paper,
To me they're sheets of white gold
Engraved with the fortunes of black onyx,
They're the treasure that can get me
Through the cost of each day
And push all my worries away.

O'mail man, please don't pass me by,
Surely a love letter would be nice,
But let it be legal mail, junk mail,
Or even impersonal spiritual mail.
Anything, and I mean anything will do.
Just as long as I know, by somebody,
I'm thought of too.   Ω

If you found me

A true friendship is a connection,
It knows no whither,
Though harsh winds may rise
And raging storms may brew,
Perfection will always shine through.
Why, out of the darkness
Two lights beam as one
In such radiance like that of the sun,
Two have become one.

A true friendship is a connection,
Then how can we be bound,
Or broken by boundaries,
Only fate could have brought us together,
If you found me.

A true friendship is a connection,
So for whatever it's worth
We can cross any line.
Why, for you I crossed the universe
Searching for love, searching for life.
I have come oh-so-close,
But never found paradise.

Trial and error burns
And comes with an awful price.
I have felt the heat
And peril of being paralyzed
Where I question my wits;
That of the trustworthy, that of the wise.
Yet from the ashes the phoenix must rise.
Broken wings must mend
And in awareness, take flight.
Take a chance, and hope to not once again ignite
Nor past the torch in anger or fright.
For to glide and soar are wonderful,
But through it all, to fly alone, what is life?

A true friendship is a connection,
So out of the darkness I part, in awareness.
Although flying blind
Searching for love, searching for life,
I trust fate and its innate light.
Why, I know when we meet
We'll gain the greatest senses of understanding
through communication.
One so powerful to run and rule a nation.
We'll be known as champions
Amongst the stars in all the constellation.

It is all worth the anticipation
For spirit attracts spirit.
So I know you were searching too,
Because a true friendship is a connection,
Then how can we be bouned
Or broken by boundaries?
Only fate could have brought us together,
If you found me.   Ω

$\mathcal{K}$ALIMA'S COMET

A comet flew across the sky
Captivating my soul as it twinkled
Within my lonesome eyes.
Why, a simple gaze into its radiant light
Offered such serenity
When all the world had offended me.
It offered a new identity
When mine was tarnished
And would hold no credibility,
It offered hope and love,
Therefore, it offered me life.

Set adrift by its celestial beauty
I became a new man
In the midst of my plight.
No, I wasn't Mike nor Ike,
But I was something sweet
In my own right.

Slowly it glided ever-so-close to my atmosphere
Whispering within my ears that
That for a lifetime I've been dying to hear.
It promised not to be like everybody else
And leave me by myself.

But to always pick me up
Through sickness and health.
In complete totality I believed
For it was not like a man
That it should lie,
Why, it was of the heavens,
Never would it severe any ties,
But in the essence of always,
It would always keep love alive.

Its awesome glow was so bright
I could see it in the day
And even in the night.
From the far east
Dark clouds started to roll in.
I could still see it,
But its shine was dim.
Over an agonizing period of time
The clouds dissipated,
Yet its glow still seemed jaded.
Nevertheless, I was entrenched
Waiting for its marvelous light to recompense.

Out over the distance
I could hear the comet's melodic voice,
But quite unusual words it began to say,
"Maybe tomorrow" and, "Not today."
As if in space, it suddenly needed space.
Desperately, I tried to reason with it,
But into the cosmos, my words went to waste.

I became broken, confused,
And in every bit of the sense misused.
For nobody wants to become

The story of yesterday's news.
My heart was torn wide open
As I realized beside
from the one true God,
promises are made to be broken.

Yet even in disarray
I was hypnotized by its regal display,
Desperately I tried to reason with it,
But again, into the cosmos
My words went to waste,
For it didn't want to hear
A word I had to say.

In all its glory
The comet begin to slowly fade,
And fade, until it completely faded away.

Astronomers say comets travel on a set course
Which can be determined as they orbit around the
Universe, therefore, maybe several years from now a twinkle
Will fill my lonesome eyes,
The same as they did the day a comet flew
Across the sky.   Ω

Everything in Jesus

I give, praise, honor, and glory
To you, O'Prince of Peace.
For when I seem unsettled,
On the very verge of being unrooted,
You comfort me.

You are…. My shield and the horn   ————— Psalm 18:2
Of my salvation, my stronghold.
How can I be bought,
How can I be broken?
If you O'Lord are my fortune
Then what is a token?
With you, is there a day I can't handle,
A day worth unhanding?
In you Jesus, I have
The peace of God,   ————— Philippians 4:7
Which surpasses all understanding…
So, no matter the way trials and tribulation
May make me stumble,
With you, on my feet is how
I will always be standing.
This peace is in my heart
And my soul.
O' I AM,

I am a light for you, O' Lord.
So awesome and amazing
Is the fruit you freely share.
From your pruning, on any days journey
I'm freshly prepared to go forth
And be fruitful that in the same
I may offer such tranquility to your children.
To all the peoples, nations, and languages
That dwell in all the earth:

Peace be multiplied to you.

Philippians 4:7

Ω

$\mathcal{M}$Y SPIRIT WILL LIVE ON

My days aren't done,
As long as I have the rise
Of the morning sun
My spirit will live on,
Ambition on the run
Even broke down under the gun,
I'm not beaten nor defeated,
My days aren't done.
By any means necessary I will fight on.

Bang!
Bang!!   Ω

DEAR MAMA

Dear Mama,
There isn't a day that goes by
That I don't miss your love, that natural born high.
The feeling is hard to explain, but I can say,
On my troubled days, thoughts of you
Or to hear the essence of love in your voice,
Helps ease my pain.
In fact I often find a smile in exchange.

There isn't a day that goes by
That I don't miss your love.
To have something so rare, precious, and beautiful
I constantly give thanks to the creator above.
Why, he gave me you, who fills my heart
More thicker than blood.
For man can't live on blood alone,
He needs that sense of warmth, comfort, and home,
That sense of tenderness when weak are his bones.
God O'God, he gave me the best mother
Man has ever known.   Ω

*A*LWAYS IN MY THOUGHTS

Home is always in my thoughts,
In my prayers, and so my dreams.
My soul pleads for it each day
Only to wake and find myself here.
But never do I lose hope
For I understand it is a war
Of spirit and flesh, mental and physical,
And I'm on the battlefield fighting
With all they place before me.

Yes, home is always in my thoughts
Which makes me a warrior fighting to get back
To all those who my thoughts wrap around;
My mom, the Lady Bug of love,
My dad, the hero that many of men never had,
My brother, that has always been by my side,
My grandfather, who became my best friend
After my sweet grandmother died,
And Ruby, my niece, who before she entered
This world knew me.
See the truth that the Holy Spirit
Is always moving.
Home is always in my thoughts
So, the fuel of my enemies I drain empty,

For I'm fueled off the joy
And blessings in each strike, each stride.
Why, home is always in my thoughts,
In my prayers, and so my dreams.
As I move swiftly fighting on Life's battlefield,
And I will not yield
Until what is in my thoughts
Has come forth and been revealed.   Ω

GREAT FRIEND, WONDERFUL GRANDFATHER

R.I.P. Grandpa 1936-2021

What will I miss?
I will miss your love, your friendship,
Your heart, you're blessing.

I will miss your ears, for I know they heard me,
Because profound lessons came moments after
In the form of a story.

I will miss your laugh, your jokes
That came to life sharing such light every time you spoke.
Although I'm a poet, you said the coldest rhymes,
Though you would modestly act like you didn't know it.
So, humble, so true, just like a real gentleman
Is known to do.

So, I will miss your concern, your support,
Your encouragement when my legs couldn't hold
And I would fall short.

I will miss your belief that I would be okay
And make it out alright,
Even though it appears I will face many more dark nights,

Yet such hope and an unimageable strength resonated
Throughout your spirit.
You knew dark times were real and coming,
But you refused to let me fear it.
What a reassurance there was in your voice
Every time I would hear it.

What a present, what a gift,
For so much was wrapped inside such a wonderful being,
Therefore, I could never choose what will I miss,
Because in truth, out of everything,
What I will miss most of all, Charles Williamson, is YOU.   Ω

MANSION OF THE MIND

(Pen-The Sword of Victory)

I open the doors
And explore all the floors.
Take a cool dip in the pool of life,
There are so many people here in my view.
I can have anything I want,
I got all I ever could need.
I step on my balcony
And there is the sun shining down on me
As if every second is all about me.
Yet selflessly I cast that glow
On others I truly love
And mean so much to me.
There is a place for them
In every room of my home.
So, on my days I feel alone
And falling apart, there are no worries.
Because the say,
"Home is where the heart is."
So, I open the doors
And explore the mansion of the mind
And they are there every time.   Ω

PSA: MY SINCEREST APOLOGIES

For those who I've wronged-
I give my sincerest apologies,
For I am truly sorry.
I have no excuse for the foundation
Of words I lay here before you,
Except to say, I stood in the deepest
Essence of wrong.

Therefore, sorrow has been my every note,
My every key, and regret my endless song
Why, there are far too many I've wronged,
As if I didn't know any better.
Regardless of whether the offense
Was little or big,
I selfishly behaved like a spoiled child,
Like a filthy little pig.

I can only hope the mental, emotional,
And physical scars have healed,
And you're not like that of the scarecrow
Who is forever stranded
In the middle of a field,
Only to be picked on externally,
But internally you've already been killed.

If I only had a brain,
I would have never been such a burden
Nor caused such pain.
Unfortunately, I can't change the past,
Though in my mind I see it everyday
As clear as glass.

No, I can't change the past,
Yet I pray you don't remain the same,
But you can find wind beneath your wings
And strength within your veins.
May you freely be able to roam
Like a wild horse without any reins.
Why, there was never any reason
For you to be tamed.

Undoubtedly the world turns round and round
And things turn and twist upside down.
Surely, I've crashed and burned
Resulting into ashes barely fit for an urn.
Yet from the ashes I arose
And was made anew.

My whole picture of life suddenly
Had a different view.
There came a overwhelming desire
To help and not hurt,
To find value and show its worth.
Although I stand on the same ground,
Under my feet, it feels like a different turf.
O' in me, God Almighty has
Surely done some work.

If I only had a brain
I would have never been such a burden
Nor caused such pain.
For I honestly had no clue
When we love and encourage,
We all can flourish,
We all can feel the goodness in our hearts
And know we have a purpose
To go forth in faith and not be nervous.

I think of all the faces I've wronged
And realize I can change
The sorrows of a sad song,
Why, with a different view
I can always emit love,
I can always pray for you.

Undoubtedly the world turns round and around
And things twist and turn upside down.
But I learned you can never
Know the plan of Him
Who wears the crown.

I pray you can forgive me
And find joy within your hearts
And on your faces, you can smile.   Ω

$\mathcal{M}$ORE ON THAT THOUGHT

Whether in a lyrical or poetic stance, rhyming is something
Like my first language. It goes back to my early childhood
Where my cousin Leron and I would go to my uncle Tommy's house.
There in his dark and nearly bare basement, with only one turntable,
A crackling mic, and speakers, we were the hottest rappers on the
Planet. (or least that's what we thought).
I say the above to simply make it clear that my apology is
Truly sincere, though brought forth in a poetic expression.
And I chose to use the reference from the Wizard of Oz,
"If I only had a brain" because, although fictitious, just like
The characters in the movie, I lived as if something significant
Was absent within my being. Of course, it was there all along,
But I made such fruitless choices. Hindsight I find no reason
Nor understanding for my actions. My youthful mind was lost and
Confused. It was full of false concepts and beliefs.
However, today, with a clear heart and mind, my eyes are wide open and
There are so many people I pray God will grant me the opportunity
To meet face to face in a desperate hope to make amends and apologize.
My circumstance holds me at bay from doing such. Nevertheless,
I take this time to grow more. I do pray this time doesn't fail us,
For life is always fleeting. If the unfortunate does occur, just
Know from the bottom of my heart, I'm sorry and I give
You my sincerest apologies.   Ω

BOYZ IN THE HOOD

Street life,
Street life,
AWAKE!
AWAKE!!!
And no longer engage,
For if you do not wake up
And turn the page,
You will end up
With more teeth than your age.   Ω

$\mathcal{A}$NOTHER CHILD

The air cleared the room
For another child is gone too soon,
Just as the release
And rise of a birthday balloon
The hour is late
And darkness beholds the moon.
For the time of death -11:50
And she was only 8   Ω

*W*HEN WILL IT STOP

Violence-
Is this some dramatic script to
A sad and hateful play?
Because in real life
War can't be the only way.

Violence-
When will it stop?
Is this our everyday harvest,
Our season's crop?
Then how shall we think to last
If numbered are our days?

Violence-
STOP! War can't be the only way.
Too many souls have passed
And in grief families have to pay.
And tears never outweigh the years
And years before their last day.
Still, we mourn them in our thoughts
And memories, those precious moments,
For that's all that's left
To hold, after death.
What a terrible lost.

Violence-
When will it stop?
WHEN WILL IT STOP?
The choice is yours.   Ω

$\mathcal{N}$EVER-BLACK

(Written with: The Sword of Force)

Stay on track my brother
Never come back.
Why, if they don't like anything,
They love the color black.
Of course they'll say it's only for criminals,
And oh yeah, the color green,
But the truth is to keep the color black
Locked up fighting in the ring
Like a wild animal in the arms
Of a untrustworthy, jailhouse legal team.
Keep the color black in ignorance,
Locked up fighting the ring
Where they may have nothing,
But unsettled dreams.
And they might not be much
But of ghetto things,
For the life of the ghetto
Is all he has ever seen.
Yet as simple and satisfying as that may seem,
If it's up to them
He'll never walk the shoes nor pants of freedom,
Not even a seam,

Those Nikes and Fubu jeans.
But why does this seem so obscene
When the color white
Rarely ever liked the color black.
Years he has broken and beaten him,
Standing on his back.
Years he has deceive and cheated him,
Justice free at that.
So, what do you think they'll do
When enforcing the color blue,
And they get their hands on you?
You'll be lucky if you're still alive
But if you turn back,
Three hots and a cot
Is how you'll surely live,
Three hots and a cot
Is how you'll surely die.
Lost to the life built
And ran by the color white,
Yes, black, plenty of brothers have made this mistake
And now it's far to late.
But if you have been here before
And have made it back to home base,
You already know all that's at stake.
Therefore, rise from all foolish things
That lead back to this chain gang,
Stay on track my brother
And never come back.
Why, if they don't like anything,
They love the color black.   Ω

MR. HATLEN & HIS LIKING

Brooks was alone
And way out of his time zone.
Why, prison became his home
And freedom became a pain
That riddled his bones.
Sadly, he gave up on life,
Because he no longer knew
Right from wrong.   Ω

$\mathcal{S}$AY SOMETHING

He needed to know he could be okay,
But you didn't say nothing.
He needed to know he could be strong,
But you didn't say nothing.
He needed to know he could make it,
But you didn't say nothing.
And now he is tragicly lost and gone,
All because you didn't say anything.

Attention
The next time you notice someone
In dire need like this, please, say something!   Ω

NOTE TO $ELF

You must turn on,
You must turn alive.
For it's the only way to live
Or else you will surely die.   Ω

UNDER THE SPOTLIGHT

I'm not a politician, not even a student of politics; in fact,
I'm not a student of much of anything. I'm not a Democrat.
I'm not a republican, and I don't even consider myself an American,
if you and I were Americans, there'd be no problem.
                            -Malcolm X, The Ballot-or-The Bullet speech-
                                                    April 3, 1964

Under the spotlight they call us
Cruel, black, senseless monsters,
Death seekers, and blood hunters,
Placing in the minds of the world
That we are worthless and to not want us.

Under the spotlight we are always wrong
No matter if we are stumped or kicked to death
They claim, "I didn't do nothing" and "What I do?"
Is our favorite song.
Probably thinking, "since you like to sing and dance
So much, well then sing on nigga, sing on."
Just look at the news, you can see it in every clip.
There is the map,
So, know I'm not sending you on a bogus trip.

It's not right, we are always wrong,
They say, "He had to do something,

He's not where he belongs.
Look at his height, his boky size,
His dark brown eyes
And the way he wears that hat."
I read between the lines
And it's like their saying, "He deserved to die,
That animal, ape,
No more of that Kool-Aid you call purple drank
When it's really grape."

It's not right, we are always wrong,
And in their hatred, they say everything
About this dead, black, child
But "His mother must be strong."
Because in truth, that was her rock, crushed and gone.
Her flower, her rising sun, her pride and joy
That she went through hard labor and pain to have him,
And you took him, her baby boy.

Under the spotlight they call us
Cruel, black, senseless monsters,
Death seekers, and blood hunters,
Placing in the minds of the world
That we are worthless and to not want us.

Now I see why it seems like
We don't have a chance.
The fight was fixed way in advance,
Hundreds of years ago when you ripped the motherland
Right out of our hands,
Being cruel, black, senseless monsters.
Times are supposed to be changed,
But now and again you smear
Martin and Malcolm's coming with your own frame,

Yet through it all we still rise.
That's what Maya Angelou was saying.

Under the spotlight we are the most hated,
Because they don't want us around,
Ironically, we are the most loved
Because they take everything from us
Claiming it as their very own,
But their version is watered down.

Under the spotlight they call us
So many things that when the truth
Is right in front of their face,
They are blind.

Well, under or out of the spotlight,
This is what I see; In us,
Surely, I've seen signs and symbols of negativity,
No doubt as I've seen in YOU!
But in us, I also see positivity, beauty,
Creativity and longevity.
We already had the presidency,
So I see strength, power, willing and wittiness.
I see humility, patience flushed with ambition.
I see hope, so I see faith and love
Built under God's grace.
I see brothers and sisters standing together in unity.
Then I see mothers and fathers tired of nonsense
And pain, for we as a world
Are supposed to be equals, we need that change.
So I see care and concern,
I see confidence and drive,
Determination with all means to stay alive.

Under the spotlight and these signs and symbols,
In us I see many things.
But most of all I see people, human beings,
I see life, I see life.
Equal and freely wanting to live,
I see LIFE.   Ω

RAYS OF LIGHT

With hope I can see through the darkness.
I can see through the cracks,
I can see as a broken man
Even in troubling times
When it's hard to be black.
For no matter the onslay
Of my dark chocolate skin,
With hope, that will never stop me
From having a vision.
It will never stop me from running forward
And going the distance.

Yes, as long as my heart beats in my chest,
It will never stop me from standing tall
And doing my best,
Even under heaps of pressure and stress.
Why, until my heart gives in,
To the fullest I will never stop liven.

With hope I can see through the darkness,
I can see light just through the cracks,
And through these cracks
I can see freedom with the light
Which is my way back.   Ω

*B*REAK THE COLOR CODE

You are white and I am black,
But that shouldn't be just that.
We have so much to offer
And share with one another
Like two brothers
Willing to make a sacred bond,
Willing to keep a sacred pact.

You are white and I am black,
But that shouldn't be just that.
We look completely different
But can share the same blood.
You may need a blood transfusion
While I may need a kidney transplant
To fix the ache and pain
Throbbing in my lower back.
And in a world full of differences
We seem to be the perfect match.

You are white and I am black,
But that shouldn't be just that.
We have children to raise
And surely, they have dreams,
Yet division is a fiendish monster

Who can kill everything.
For it rains such destruction,
Not leaving a seam nor a crack
In the wake of its brutal attack,
Except in pushing humanity
Further and further back.

But why should we let this legendary
American nightmares have any of that?
Surely, we have the power to upstage him,
And snuff out his final act
By simply teaching our children
How to grow together as a team.
We would combine such a natural force
Capable to take on anything
Like two brothers
Willing to make a sacred bond,
Willing to keep a sacred pact,
All because you are white
And I am black,
Now that could be just that!   Ω

OUR WORLD (MOTHER EARTH)

She was cold and subdued
With bad fruit revealed,
Leaving no hidden truth.

She was cold and subdued,
Man, death really knows how to kill.
For she was raped, scarred,
And smothered by fumes.
Peculiarly she often found herself
Staring jealously at the vacant moon,
Wanting that same fate
As if she was praying for tomorrow's doom.

She was cold and subdued,
Clothed less than tatters,
She roamed aimlessly in the nude,
Ripped and torn, it hurt to the core.
Left with a polluted and ruined womb
Expectations were slim if anything
Could still be born.
Or would it reap the devastation
Of becoming stillborn?

She was cold and subdued,
Man, death really knows how to kill.
Why, here lies a dethroned queen,
A run-down mother,
No good to her children
Because they were no good to their mother.   Ω

THE TALK-OR-A DIFFERENT KIND OF TALK

I wanted to tell my son
About the birds and the bees,
But I had to tell him about Covid-19
And the spread of sickness and disease.

I wanted to tell my son
He was young and full of life,
But I had to tell him
Death can come at any moment,
Even in the middle of the night.

I wanted to tell my son
It's okay, you have friends and family
Who will stand by your side,
But I had to tell him
To use social media,
Send a text or a tweet
For too many have already passed.
And in hospitals, nobody can be there
When you die.

I wanted to tell my son
About many of things, but instead,

I hugged him tightly in my arms
And speechless, I just cried.
Because besides my love for him,
I was uncertain about anything,
Even if this was our last time
To say, "Good-bye."   Ω

*T*O THE OUTSIDE WORLD

Wrote = 4/18/2020

I have walked these halls
And smelt the putrid fumes of rage.
Some even called me by my name,
But I refused to engage.

I have walked these halls,
It started at the age 21, now I'm 34,
That's 13 years, yet I refuse to count the days.
The truth is, there is plenty more time left
If I shall have to stay.

I have walked these halls,
Surely, I've been through somethings
So ultimately I've changed.
I want to say, "but the bricks remain the same."
Yet they too have changed
And become filled with cracks,
The wear and tear of unfair time.
You can also see it in my face,
Why, together we've aged, and so we match.

I have walked these halls
And in this direction, I can never

Get my grandmother nor my brother back.
For they have gone to the grave,
And with the living so much time has expired
In which that neither will I ever get back.

I have walked these halls
And have met a few good men
Who have taught me how to stand tall,
While many other showed me
They would stab me right in my back.

I have walked these walls
And amongst my peril
I found my hidden talent.
This would settle the heavy tides
And give me some kind of balance,
So within these halls I wrote
And wrote so many poetic pieces
I could have my own version of "Gun Smoke."

I have walked these halls,
Although I'm surrounded by bricks upon bricks
And the coiling barbwire fence,
I broke through these walls without touching them.
Why, withing my darkness I beheld magic,
For a lonely road always has a hat trick.

I have walked these halls
Yet I found myself in front of Rock Island
Schools and city hall protesting for a little girl,
Screaming, "Justice For Jasper!"
Though I threw my ball
And struck out with a curve,
I found sparks of love that I didn't deserve.

It's electric filled my finger tips
And trickled up and down my nerves.
Sadly, as good as it felt
It was just a power surge.
No fuss nor fright though anger did ignite,
I must continue on as a humble bird.

I have walked these halls
And I've been told my poetry is great,
But I don't have one award to show that weight.
That's okay that's alright
Because I have been on a thousand adventures
In just one sleepless night.
I have walked these halls
And remember Yusaf, who is serving NATURAL LIFE.
Mastering the law he bobbed and weaved,
Still the state said if it's up to them
They'll have his last breath
Whenever it shall breathe.
But I wonder did he know
He gave me possibly the last or at least
One of the coldest tricks up his sleeve.

I have walked these halls
Now in my darkest hour I run
Racing to reach the top of the tower
Before they can stop me from throwing my work
To the outside world.
That at least it will be free, my brother,
Even if we shall never leave.   Ω

My LONELY ROAD

I can't say my feet hurt,
But boy, they sure have put in some work.
Caught in the obscene ways of life
And the obscure essence of time,
The perilous walk-through miles of filth and dirt.
For whatever was the worth,
Out of it birth this path, my journey.
The seconds, minutes, hours, days
That between standing spears turned to long harsh years
Roaming aimlessly without a sufficient cure.

I wanted a way out,
Yet only darkness I could find,
Only darkness I endured.
I thought to let my soul burn.
And though a soul can waste away,
As long as life is in it,
It can't burn up in flames.
Yet it can know suffering, know shame,
And be clouded deep within the night's midst,
Shrouded by darkness as a sky's stormy domain
Just before the vigorous rain.
Witness such a dreadful walk-through life's faulty terrain.
I can't say my feet hurt,

But boy, they sure have put in some work.
I wanted a way out,
A savior in these times of disaster, these times of pain,
There to help defeat the storms, the hurricanes.
Someone, anyone, but only tears came.

Hopeless, broken a heart torn wide and open
In a catastrophic explosion.
The perilous walk-through miles of filth and dirt,
The feeling to have no one there when it truly hurts.

I admit, I once had many things,
But burned them up with the fuel of selfishness
And hate's flame.
Yet as a human being, I miss them all the same,
Someone, anyone of them, but only tears came.

Going through all these changes
I felt danger instead of dangerous.
Such deterioration of character
But not just into ashes nor dust,
Worn to weakness, I felt discomfort
At the slightest stroke of a brush.
Alone, so alone,
In the mind, me, and myself
Toiled and tussled screaming,
"JUST GIVE UP!"
But I wanted a way out.
So much desperation for the slightest
Comfort of warmth when I looked to the sun
For its reflecting shine,
Only darkness was there bending up my spine.
All my focus was obliterated,
Shooting pain knocked me blind.

Drifting in and out of consciousness
With what remained of common sense,
I called out in the darkness
But no meaningful answer came,
Not even shadows of the solo dancer.
Nothing but nothingness,
Though I begged, prayed, plead,
And even sent sincere letters of apologies.

Nevertheless, only darkness answered.
And though black ink is what I spill
In expression, confessions,
And such words of vital essence,
I did not want to fall into his well.
Why, I know he only deceives
For he was there bending up my spine.
All my focus was obliterated,
Shooting pain knocked me blind.

My hands tied, unable to rewind time,
The seconds, minutes, hours, days
That between standing spears turned to years.
Caught in the obscene ways of life
And the obscure essence of time,
I wanted a way out,
Someone there, willing to share
That feeling of warmth and home.
Yet by myself I remain,
By myself I still roam.

Then can I start over on a clean slate
Or is this darkness really my twisted fate?
However, without a base to stand on,
Ironically, I found home plate.

The perilous walk-through miles of filth and dirt,
When there was nobody to acknowledge me
Holding up my sign for help, my SOS.
It was then I found myself
Travelling on my lonely road.

The End   Ω

NEVERTHELESS

HEY

PUBLISHER

ℳ POETRY

This piece was supposed to be no more than a catchy cover
Letter to grab the attention of publishers. But a poem was born.
To whomever may be of assistance

Time and time again I've been told
my poetry is like the Almighty's loving clutch.
Why, from heart to heart they surely have been touch.
For within simple words, they have found ways
And meaning that meant so much.
That when they were on the floor,
They were able to get up, stand, then soar,
Making that meaning so much more.

Time and time again I've been told
That I couldn't have written any of this.
"Life Of the Wild"
-or-
"Girl Have You Ever Truly Been Kissed"
Fitting such words in a style so quotish,
For within simple words focused, they have found ways
and meaning that meant so much. I've noticed.
"No, these are the words of a great author,
The passionate words of a great poet." They often insist.
"Whose work has been copy-written,

Stamped, bound, published then to the stores once printed.
Such as, scholastic and Kingfish.
In fact, you just spent time to copy all of this."

Time and time again I'm flattered by all they say.
Compliments have even helped me in moments
And times when I myself felt I could shatter.
Break to pieces,
Beauty no more a matter.
Break to pieces,
That beauty is no more a fine display.
Even if they didn't believe it was me
There was no dismay.

On and on the ink poured
Giving all my mind would let.
Dueling myself in a challenge, we made a bet!
Me and I, I and me.
Yet like this, no longer can things stay.
So here and now I look to you,
Searching for away,
What route to take and travel?
What hills to make to avoid faulty battle?
Please tell me what proper way
Do I need to come to you.
So I can get things copy-written
Stamped, bound, published then printed
All this poetry that spills from my mind
In harden times when I vent.

So that, time and time again
When a poem touches someone's heart
And heals suffering and shame,
They can look to a cover and say,

"Terrance J. Williamson,
That is the author and poet
Who healed my pain."
They can look up and say,
"Terrance J. Williamson,
That is your name!"

$\mathcal{M}$ORE COMING SOON BY THIS AUTHOR

* The Earth and All Its Goodness
    Featuring Poem "Kids of the Class"
* Children's Book
    The Best Unspoken Words
* And more such as:
    -Gospel Music
    -Jiggles
    -Spiritual Book

$\mathcal{F}$RIENDS AND FANS CAN CONTACT THIS AUTHOR AT:

Write
Terrance J. Williamson #R48362
Centralia Correctional Center
P.O. Box 7711
Centralia, Illinois 62801

Or

Email
Connect Network.com
Terrance J. Williamson R48362

SPECIAL THANKS

To God for loving me no matter what and giving me the gift of poetry to relate, uplift, and encourage others.

Thank you for sending me an angel, Isabel Montaño from Hebrews 13:3 Prison Ministry who lit the way.

To my mother who gives me strength that only a mother can give.

To my dad and grandfather who will always be unshakable pillars in my life.

To my aunt Naomi who knows how to be a true friend.

And last, but not least, all who are in my corner. You know who you are.

Thank you.

Printed in the United States
by Baker & Taylor Publisher Services